Park

Deni Bown

Illustrated by Wendy Meadway

Through the Seasons

Field and Hedgerow
Garden
Park
Pond
Stream
Wood

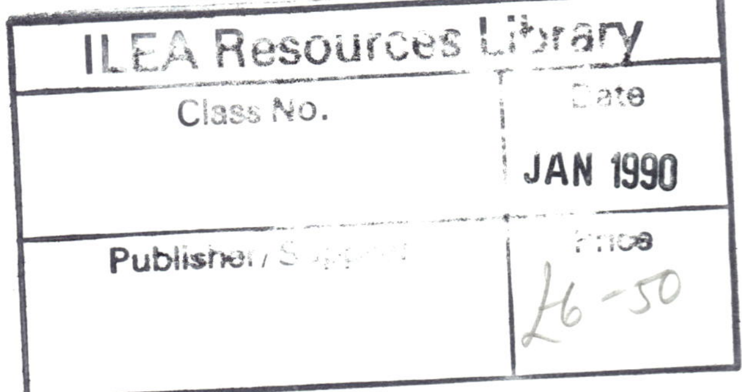

Edited by Sarah Doughty
Series design by Charles Harford HSD
Book design by Ross George

First published in 1989 by
Wayland (Publishers) Ltd
61 Western Road, Hove
East Sussex BN3 1JD, England

© Copyright 1989 Wayland (Publishers) Ltd

British Library Cataloguing in Publication Data
Bown, Deni
  Park.
  I. Title   II. Meadway, Wendy   III. Series
  574.5'2

ISBN 1 85210 763 4

Phototypeset by D.P. Press, Sevenoaks, Kent
Printed in Italy by G. Canale & C.S.p.A., Turin
Bound in Belgium by Casterman, S.A.

CONTENTS

Words that appear in **bold** in the text
are explained in the glossary on page 30.

WHAT IS A PARK?

Parks are places where everyone can go for walks.

In every park there are open spaces of grass, fine trees and beautiful gardens. Most parks are owned by the town or city and are looked after by a special Parks Department. They are there for everyone to enjoy.

You can play games in the park, have a picnic, or sit and look at the plants and animals that live there. Parks are especially important in cities, where few people have large gardens and the countryside is far away.

In large parks there are areas of natural woodland.

As well as colourful flowerbeds and tidy lawns, many parks have natural areas of grass and woodland. In places which are undisturbed, there is a greater variety of living things. These include birds and insects, a few frogs or toads, and perhaps some **mammals**, such as hedgehogs and wood mice. Even foxes and squirrels may live there.

On the lake there are ducks, geese and swans to feed.

Some of the birds on the lake live there all year round. Others visit the lake from time to time, especially in winter when food is hard to find. The commonest **waterfowl** are mallard ducks. The female is brown, and the male has a green head, white neck and purple-brown breast. Male ducks are called drakes.

Magnolia trees flower before the new leaves appear.

The spring-flowering magnolias are slow-growing **deciduous** trees which bloom when the branches are still bare. Their large, scented white or pink flowers are so beautiful that many people go to the park especially to see them.

The laburnum tree has yellow flowers. Its seeds are poisonous.

The laburnum is also called the golden rain tree because of its long chains of yellow flowers. After the flowers have fallen, the seed pods begin to grow. The seeds look like small peas in a pea pod but they, like all parts of the tree, are poisonous.

Horse chestnut flowers stand up above the leaves.

In early spring the sticky buds of the horse chestnut tree open into new leaves. Each leaf has five to seven **leaflets**. When the leaves are fully grown, the upright clusters of flowers open. They have white petals with yellow and pink spots, and long curved **stamens**. From a distance it looks as if someone has decorated the tree with candles!

Sycamore trees have dangling green flowers.

When the wind blows **pollen** from the male flowers to the female flowers, winged seeds begin to develop. Sycamores have large hand-shaped leaves, with five points. Sometimes they become covered in black spots. This is a **fungus** which damages the leaves. The leaves may also be eaten by the caterpillars of the sycamore moth.

The flowerbeds are full of tulips and wallflowers in the spring.

Twice a year the gardeners change the plants in the smaller flowerbeds. In the autumn they plant tulips, wallflowers, pansies, hyacinths and polyanthus, which flower in spring. When these have finished flowering, the gardeners fill the beds with summer bedding plants which last until the autumn. They choose exciting colours and plant the beds in neat rows.

◄ Birds build their nests in quiet corners of the park.

The trees, bushes and wilder parts of the park are home to many different birds, such as robins (in the picture), pigeons, house sparrows, starlings, blackbirds, chaffinches and blue tits. Some of them are very tame, as they are used to people feeding them.

THINGS TO DO IN SPRING

Go for a walk in the park with your family or friends and decide which is your favourite tree. Find out what it is called and make a study of it. Keep a special notebook, describing all the details: its shape, the bark, twigs, leaves, flowers and fruits. Draw each part and notice how the tree changes with the seasons.

Ask for a bag of food for the birds. Stale bread will do but even better is the proper bird food which is sold in pet shops and garden centres. If you sit quietly on a seat in the park and throw a little at a time, more and more birds will come to feed. See how many you can **identify**. If there are any that you cannot recognize, look them up in a guide book in the library. In late spring, parent birds may bring their young with them.

The swan is a graceful water bird often seen in parks.

◄ Rose gardens are lovely places to visit in summer.

Some parks have a rose garden. Roses flower all summer and their brightly-coloured, fragrant flowers are very popular. There are many different kinds. Some are named after people or places. If you look at the labels in a rose garden you should be able to find out their names.

Some parks have gardens for disabled people. ►

In gardens for the disabled, paths are level and wide enough for wheelchairs to pass each other. The flowerbeds are raised up so that the plants are easy to reach. The plants are chosen carefully. Those with scented flowers, **aromatic** leaves and interesting textures bring pleasure to blind people.

Gardeners can make beautiful patterns with flowers.

Some parks have flowerbeds planted in a way which is called carpet bedding. At a distance they look like a patterned carpet. The plants are arranged so that they make numbers, letters or shapes.

They are planted so close together that no soil can be seen between them, and they remain very small even when flowering. In the picture you can see a butterfly made from red, pink and white flowers.

There are daisies and other plants growing in the grass.

Every park has large areas of grass. Some of it is cut short so that we can walk, play or sit on it. In places where it is left to grow long, the grasses and other plants reach their full height and flower. You can then see how many different kinds of plants it takes to make grassland.

◄ Daisies flower even when the grass is cut.

Although grassland is made up of different kinds of grasses, large numbers of daisies grow among them. Because the leaves of daisy plants lie close to the soil they are not damaged by mowing. The short-stalked flowers grow very quickly and open before the grass is cut again.

Yarrow is a tough plant with feathery leaves and small leaflets.

Yarrow plants spread through the grass by wiry underground stems. It is a tough plant which is not harmed by trampling and mowing. Even if some of the leaflets are damaged, there are plenty more which survive.

◄ The flowers of germander speedwell appear when the grass is not cut.

Germander speedwell grows in patches among other grassland plants. Its small leaves are hard to see on short grass, but as soon as the grass grows long, the speedwell's stems grow upwards and bear tiny bright blue flowers.

Canada geese graze on lawns in the park.

The Canada goose now lives and **breeds** in Britain, but originally came from North America. It was brought to this country over a century ago as an **ornamental** bird for lakes in parks. Canada geese live in flocks of up to 300 birds. They nest together beside the lake and eat mostly grass.

Both parent coots feed their young.

▶

Coots are quite small water birds that work together to build a large nest of reeds in the lake. They both sit on their eggs and look after their chicks. They also repair the nest and find food for their family.

You may see some of these waterfowl in your park.

Some common insects and spiders.

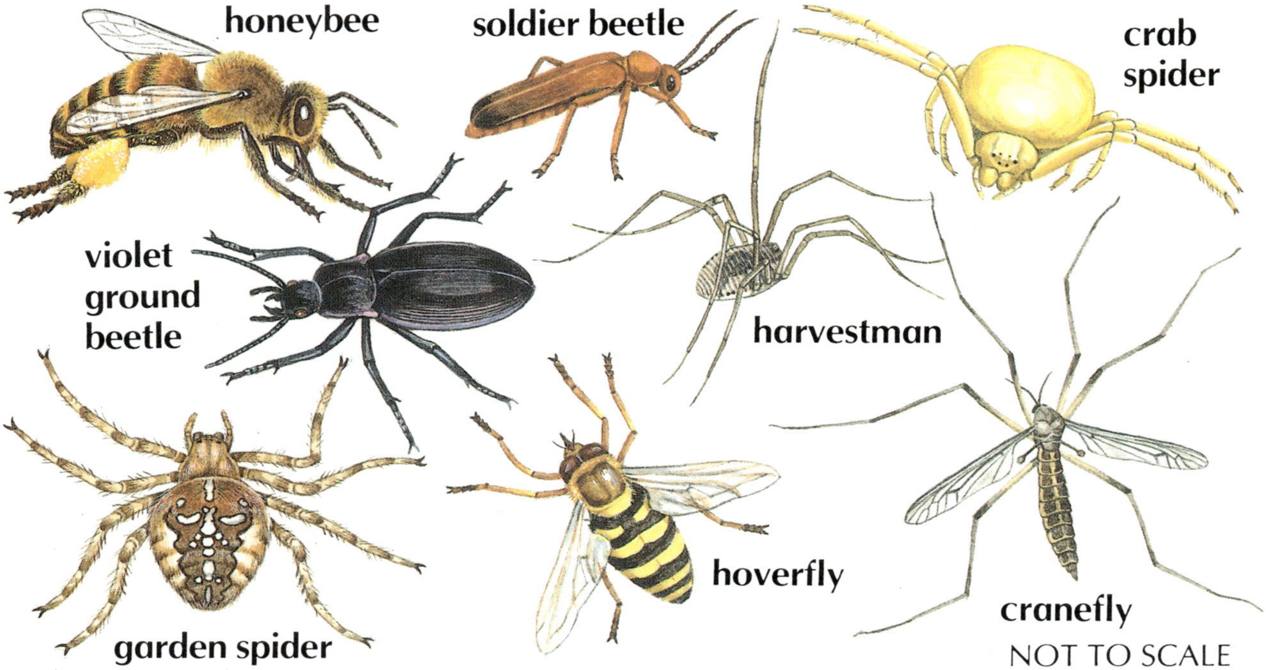

honeybee

soldier beetle

crab spider

violet ground beetle

harvestman

garden spider

hoverfly

cranefly

NOT TO SCALE

Wolf spiders like to sit in the sun among the flowers. ▶

The wolf spider is found in flowerbeds. It can often be seen sitting on warm stones, leaves or flowers in full sun. In early summer the females carry a round **cocoon** of eggs. When the eggs hatch, the young spiders ride around on their mother's back for the first few days.

Bumblebees are larger and more colourful than honeybees.

There are always large furry bumblebees buzzing around the flowers in summer. They are collecting **nectar** and pollen to feed to the **grubs** in their nest. At the same time they are **pollinating** the flowers. Bumblebees build nests of grass and moss under the ground, often in the old nests of mice or voles. Unlike honeybees, they do not store honey to feed themselves through the winter. In the autumn, the old **queen** bumblebees and the **worker bees** die, leaving only the new queens to **hibernate** through the winter.

The life cycle of a wasp.

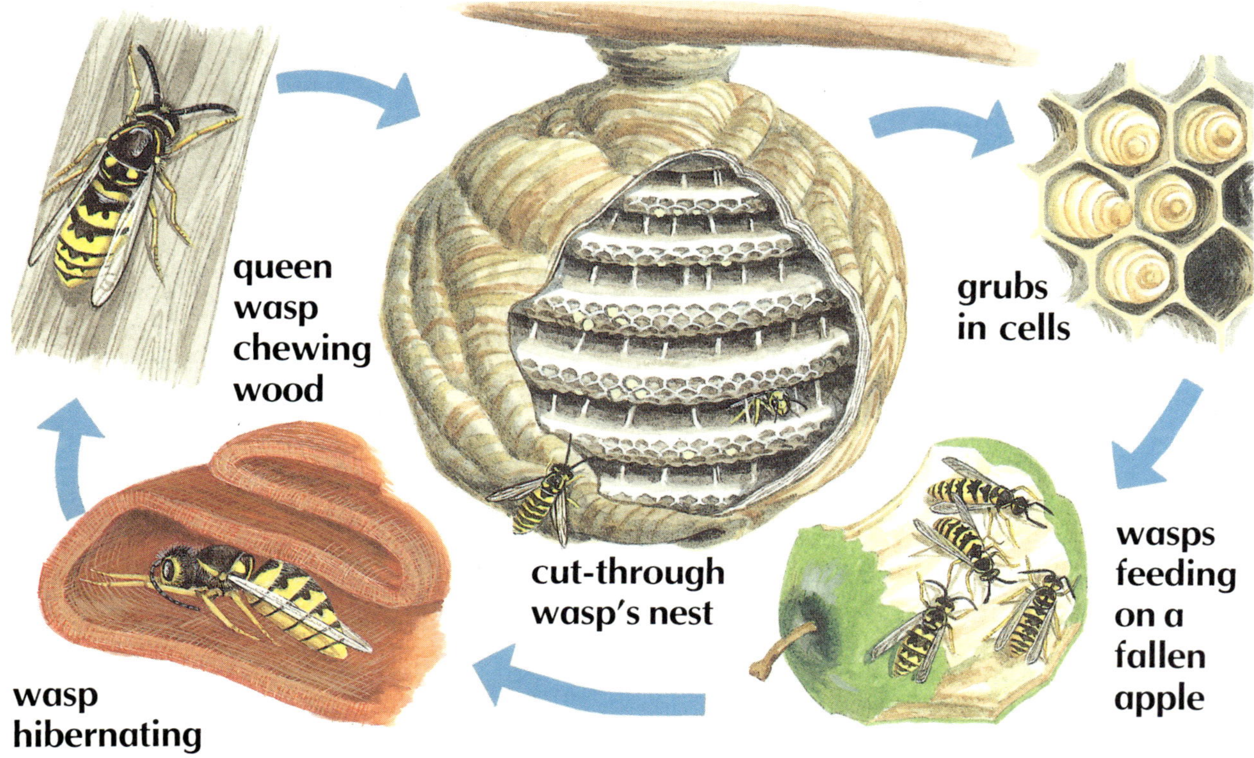

Like bumblebees, wasps live in **colonies** which last only a year. Each spring, the young queens come out of hibernation and build papery nests from chewed-up wood. The nest is large, and by midsummer it may contain 2,000 wasps. During the spring and summer, wasps kill caterpillars and insects by stinging them, and take them back to the nest to feed the grubs. In late summer when the last grubs hatch, they stop hunting insects and spend more time feeding on sugar. Wasps can often be seen in kitchens and around picnic sites, attracted by the smell of jam and other sweet foods.

THINGS TO DO IN SUMMER

If there is a lake in the park near where you live, see if you can identify the waterfowl on it. When you know which are which, keep a record of how many of each kind you can see each time you go. You may find that the number of waterfowl varies greatly through the year, especially at the change of the seasons.

There are more insects in summer than at any other time of the year. We get used to seeing bees buzzing around flowers, but to see exactly what they are doing you have to get very close and watch very carefully. If a bee is collecting pollen, you can see it scrape the powder from the stamens of the flower and pack it into tiny pouches on its legs. Butterflies have long thin tongues which they unroll to reach into the flower and suck nectar. Creep up and spy on the insects to see what they are doing when they land on flowers.

The word daisy means the eye of the day because it opens its flowers at dawn and closes them as darkness falls. When you next go to the park, find some daisies – day's eyes – in the grass and try to make a daisy chain. You need sharp fingernails to do this as you have to make a slit in the stalk of each daisy to thread the next one through. As you sit making your daisy chain, think up a poem about daisies.

Try to make a daisy chain.

Some trees turn red in the autumn.

Many of the deciduous trees and shrubs in the park, such as these cherry trees and Japanese maples, are planted specially for their autumn colours. They lose all their leaves in the autumn so that they are not damaged by freezing weather. Before the leaves fall, the food in them slowly goes back into the twigs. When this happens, the leaves change colour. As each leaf falls, it makes a scar where the stalk was joined to the twig.

The berries of the snowberry bush are like large white pearls.

Falling leaves and ripe fruits make autumn one of the most colourful times of the year. Some bushes and trees are grown specially for their brightly-coloured berries. You may see birds eating berries from plants in the park but they are not safe for you to eat.

Tortoiseshell butterflies feed on the last flowers of the autumn.

The tortoiseshell butterfly lays its eggs on nettles. They hatch into black caterpillars which spin webs among the leaves to protect themselves while feeding. When they reach their full size, they **pupate** and two weeks later emerge as butterflies. As soon as the weather turns cold in autumn, they find somewhere sheltered to hibernate.

Sycamore trees have winged fruits which spin as they fall.

The wings of sycamore fruits are rather like the blades of a helicopter. Instead of falling straight to the ground, the wind catches the wings and makes them spin round. This carries them further away from the parent tree so that they have more space to grow.

◄ The prickly fruits of the horse chestnut split open when they fall.

The horse chestnut tree has large shiny brown seeds which are known as conkers. When they fall, they land under the parent tree, but many of them are taken away by animals such as squirrels. Some conkers are eaten, but a few may be left to **germinate** in the spring.

Squirrels gather conkers and acorns from under the trees.

In the autumn, there is plenty of food for all the birds and mammals in the park. They eat as much as they can so that they are strong enough to live through the winter.

Some animals, such as squirrels and wood mice, also collect nuts and seeds and store them in secret places so that they have enough to eat on cold winter days.

THINGS TO DO IN AUTUMN

Ask someone for a very large piece of paper about a metre square. You could use two lengths of plain wallpaper joined together with Sellotape. Draw a tree with bare branches.

Next, collect as many different autumn leaves as you can find under the trees in the park (only one or two from each tree). Press them between sheets of newspaper, weighed down with a pile of books, for a few days. Then glue them on to the paper, as if they are falling from the tree in autumn. When they are all in place, write the name of the tree next to its leaf.

The autumn leaves of the Japanese maple are red.

You could collect cherry leaves to press and keep.

In winter, gulls move into towns to find food.

You may see seagulls on park grassland in the winter. The seagull in the picture is a herring gull. You may also see black-headed gulls. Their winter **plumage** is white but for the rest of the year their heads are black. The gulls like to roost in open spaces such as park lawns. Soon after sunrise each day, they fly off to feed. Gulls are mainly **scavengers** and often feed from rubbish tips.

Starlings perch noisily in the trees.

Starlings live in large flocks, feeding together and flying home to the same **roost** every evening. In the winter, it is easy to see them perching in the bare trees. They are noisy birds and make a wide range of sounds, including calls and whistles which they copy from other birds – or even from people. Starlings eat almost anything they can find: worms, slugs, snails, spiders, insects, seeds and fruit.

Crocuses open wide in the late winter sunshine.

Few plants flower in winter. There are not many insects to pollinate them and the pollen might be ruined by rain. Those plants that do flower in winter are good at protecting themselves. Crocuses shut tightly when it is cloudy or wet, keeping the pollen warm and dry inside. When it brightens up, they open quickly and show their brilliant colours.

THINGS TO DO IN WINTER

Winter is one of the most interesting times of the year for watching waterfowl. Unusual birds such as the tufted duck are attracted by the good supply of food in ponds and lakes. At the same time, some birds leave the lake to spend the winter somewhere warmer. You may see the Canada geese flying off in a 'V' shape, heading for the coast. If you began to keep a record of the waterfowl in the summer, now is the time to be especially watchful. You may see some interesting birds among the more common ones.

When the deciduous trees and bushes have lost their leaves, the park looks very different. You can see buildings and views that were previously hidden by **foliage**. However, some trees and bushes keep their leaves in winter. They are called evergreens. Next time you go for a walk in the park, notice how many different evergreens there are. In particular, see if you can

Mistletoe is an evergreen plant with white berries.

find those that we cut for Christmas decorations: holly, ivy, mistletoe, and **conifers** such as spruce which we use as Christmas trees. Mistletoe will be the hardest one to find. It is a **parasite** that lives on certain trees. If you look high into the branches of apple and poplar trees in winter, you may see huge bunches of mistletoe growing from the bare branches.

Spring
Summer

Autumn
Winter

GLOSSARY

Aromatic Having a strong and interesting smell (for example, mint).

Bedding plants Short-lived plants for flowerbeds.

Breeds Produces young.

Cocoon A silky covering which protects the developing young of certain animals (for example, the eggs of spiders).

Colonies Groups of the same kind of animal living together.

Conifer A tree which bears cones.

Deciduous Trees that lose all their leaves at the end of the growing season.

Foliage The green leaves of plants.

Fungus A plant which has no leaves, stems, roots or flowers, and lives on other plants or animals (for example, mushrooms, and toadstools).

Germinate To begin to grow.

Grubs The young, or larvae, of some insects.

Hibernate To spend the winter in a sleep-like state.

Identify To find out the name of a plant or animal.

Leaflets Small leaves which form part of a bigger leaf.

Mammals Animals which feed their young on milk.

Nectar A sugary liquid produced by flowers.

Ornamental Something that is beautiful, kept because it is nice to look at.

Parasite A plant or animal that lives and feeds either on or in another one.

Plumage A bird's feathers.

Pollen Powder produced by the male parts of a flower which makes the female parts develop seeds.

Pollinating Carrying pollen from the male parts of a flower to the female parts.

Pupate To turn into a chrysalis (a hardened case in which grubs change into adult insects).

Queen The only female bee (or wasp) in a colony that can lay eggs.

Roost A place where birds rest or sleep.
Scavengers Animals that eat left-over or decaying food.
Stamens The male parts of a flower.

Waterfowl Birds which live on fresh water (for example, ducks, geese and swans).
Worker bees The female bees in a colony that search for food and feed the young bees.

BOOKS TO READ

Discovering Bees and Wasps by C. O'Toole (Wayland, 1985).
Discovering Ducks, Geese and Swans by Tony Wharton (Wayland, 1987).
Discovering Spiders by Malcolm Penny (Wayland, 1985).
In the Park by Ralph Whitlock (Wayland, 1986).

Look around the Park by C. Pace & J. Birch (Wayland, 1988).
My Class Visits a Park by Vicki Lee (Franklin Watts, 1985).
The Life Cycle of a Duck by Jill Bailey (Wayland, 1988).
Who Hides in a Park? by Warabe Aska (Ragged Bear, 1988).

Picture acknowledgements
All photographs were taken by Deni Bown with the exception of the following: Chris Fairclough Colour Library 8 (left), 17, 23, 25 (both), A.E. Wills 12 (left).

INDEX